AN INSIDER'S LOOK AT THE NORTH KOREAN REGIME

HEARING

BEFORE THE

COMMITTEE ON FOREIGN AFFAIRS
HOUSE OF REPRESENTATIVES

ONE HUNDRED FIFTEENTH CONGRESS

FIRST SESSION

NOVEMBER 1, 2017

Serial No. 115–78

Printed for the use of the Committee on Foreign Affairs

Available via the World Wide Web: http://www.foreignaffairs.house.gov/ or
http://www.gpo.gov/fdsys/

U.S. GOVERNMENT PUBLISHING OFFICE

27–389PDF   WASHINGTON : 2017

For sale by the Superintendent of Documents, U.S. Government Publishing Office
Internet: bookstore.gpo.gov   Phone: toll free (866) 512–1800; DC area (202) 512–1800
Fax: (202) 512–2104   Mail: Stop IDCC, Washington, DC 20402–0001

CONTENTS

AN INSIDER'S LOOK AT THE NORTH KOREAN REGIME

WEDNESDAY, NOVEMBER 1, 2017

House of Representatives,
Committee on Foreign Affairs,
Washington, DC.

The committee met, pursuant to notice, at 10:30 a.m., in room 2172 Rayburn House Office Building, Hon. Edward Royce (chairman of the committee) presiding.

Chairman ROYCE. This hearing will come to order. All members, if you will have your seats.

Thae Yong-ho is one of the highest-ranking North Korean officials ever to defect. As this former Deputy Ambassador to the United Kingdom will tell us, he wanted his family to be free. It is rare that we have the opportunity to hear from someone with such unique insight into the most repressive regime in the world and one that is now threatening us with nuclear weapons.

Mr. Thae, I wanted to say thank you for speaking before this committee today and wanted also to acknowledge that it takes courage for you to do this.

I met with you in August in Seoul, along with Mr. Yoho of this committee and Mr. Schneider and Mr. Bera. Your observations and your recommendations to the committee today will not only help inform U.S. policy, but it is my hope that your message, including how we can peacefully denuclearize the Korean Peninsula, will reach the ears of every North Korean still suffering under Kim Jong-un's brutal rule.

As I know you agree, it is crucial that we get information to North Koreans so that they can better understand the corruption of the self-serving regime there. As we will hear, elites live in relative luxury while millions barely survive. Our efforts are already putting pressure on the regime by creating and increasing defections from the country. I think the Kim regime is vulnerable.

To support our information efforts, the House recently passed legislation authored by Chairman Emeritus Ros-Lehtinen to reauthorize the North Korean Human Rights Act. This important bill continues our broadcasts and it updates our efforts to include more modern technology to help spread outside information into North Korea. While we should take a diplomatic approach to North Korea, the reality is that the regime itself will never be at peace with its people, its neighbors, or us.

But information is not our only tool. Congress also has done its part to ramp up economic pressure. We passed my North Korea

Sanctions bill last February. In July, we increased the tools at the administration's disposal by passing a big sanctions package, which targets, among other things, North Korean slave labor.

In August, the administration secured a major victory with the unanimous adoption of U.N. Security Council Resolution 2371. Myself and Mr. Engel saw Ambassador Nikki Haley last night. Ambassador Haley called this "the strongest sanctions ever imposed in response to a ballistic missile test." And in September, under her leadership, the Security Council passed another resolution, further upping the pressure on the regime in response to its sixth nuclear test.

To be effective, these tools must be implemented aggressively. We will hear today how sanctions are having an impact and hurting the regime there. The administration has increased the pace, but we need to dramatically increase the number of North Korean-related designations, and we need to do that without delay.

By using all the tools at our disposal, we can bring the necessary pressure to bear peacefully in order to denuclearize the Korean Peninsula. Mr. Thae, your insights into the impact of these efforts and life in North Korea will be invaluable and I thank you for joining us here today.

I have been in North Korea once. Mr. Engel has been there on two occasions, and I want to thank the ranking member. What we are going to do now, Mr. Thae, is he will have his opening statement.

Then we will go to you and we will hear from you, and afterwards we will go to the members of the committee so that they might ask you questions and then you can respond.

Mr. Engel, if you would like to make your opening statement.

Mr. ENGEL. Thank you very much, Mr. Chairman, and I stand by every word you said in your opening statement. We have no disagreement on this very important issue.

Mr. Thae, welcome to the Foreign Affairs Committee. We are deeply grateful for your time this morning. As the chairman said, several members of the committee, myself included, have visited North Korea. I have been there twice, but not lately.

We have had dozens and dozens of diplomats and experts appear before us to discuss our strategy for dealing with Pyongyang, to shed light on the abuses of the Kim regime, to provide insight on North Korea's development of nuclear weapons.

You know, one of the things that was interesting when I was in Pyongyang is I got up early in the morning and walked around and we saw a lot of people going to work, and they looked well fed. They looked well dressed. Everything was fine.

I was then told that—by others that these were the elites and the only ones in North Korea that are functioning well and they kept us out of any place other than Pyongyang. They didn't want us to see what was going on in the rest of the country.

So the insight you can provide, Mr. Thae, will give our members and the public a unique perspective on this challenge. You come to us at an urgent time. Obviously, the Kim regime has accelerated its development of nuclear weapons and ways to deliver them.

Our allies—South Korea and Japan—are at risk and the day is quickly approaching when North Korea will have the ability to hit the United States with a devastating nuclear payload.

Any conflict on the Korean Peninsula, nuclear or conventional, would entail horrific loss of life. This is one of the most urgent challenges we face on the global stage—no doubt about it.

And let's call it the way we see it. Administrations of both parties have failed to put a lid on the Kim regime's nuclear program over the course of decades.

But I feel that what's happening now—the President and the administration are undermining diplomacy in North Korea, where it is needed more than ever, hampering our ability to lead on the issue.

The strategy that key cabinet officials laid out seems to call for a combination of multilateral, diplomatic, and economic pressure. These policies, along with shows of military force like flying bombers in South Korean airspace, are aimed at slowing North Korea's advances.

I am not sure we have seen evidence of that. Unfortunately, what we have seen is rising tensions between Washington and Pyongyang.

Kim's rhetoric and the President's rhetoric has thrown fuel on the fire and I believe it has escalated the risk of conflict. Let me just say, as I've said before, more than 9 months into this administration we still have no Assistant Secretary of State for East Asia and the Pacific, no Under Secretary for Arms Control and International Security, no Ambassador to South Korea, and I worry what may happen later on in this month when the President travels to Asia.

So there is lots and lots of work to be done and I am glad that this committee is staying focused on this issue. I hope we will hear from the administration again soon on its path forward.

This is especially important in light of the many senior level discussions with allies and partners in Asia due to take place over the next few weeks in conjunction with the President's trip.

So I'll wrap up because I want to make sure most of our time today is spent hearing from our witness. Again, we are fortunate to have you, Mr. Thae, with us today.

Thank you, Mr. Chairman. I yield back.

Chairman ROYCE. Thank you, Mr. Engel.

So this morning, members, we are pleased to be joined by Mr. Thae Yong-Ho. He is the former Deputy Chief of Mission, Embassy of the People's Republic of Korea in the United Kingdom.

As a former high-ranking North Korean official, Mr. Thae can provide us, I think, some unique insights into Kim Jong-un's regime. And so without objection, the witness' full prepared statements will be made part of the record. Members are going to have 5 calendar days to submit any statements or questions or any extraneous material for the record here today.

And, Mr. Thae, if you would summarize your remarks, the floor is yours. Thank you, Mr. Thae. Yes.

STATEMENT OF MR. THAE YONG-HO (FORMER DEPUTY CHIEF OF MISSION, EMBASSY OF THE DEMOCRATIC PEOPLE'S REPUBLIC OF KOREA IN THE UNITED KINGDOM)

Mr. THAE. Chairman Royce, Ranking Member Engel, distinguished members of the House committee, thank you for the opportunity to be here today.

First, I would like to express my sincere gratitude to Chairman Royce who kept his promise to accommodate my wishes to visit the United States and gave me this opportunity to testify before the House Committee on Foreign Affairs.

As you are all aware, I worked at the front line of North Korean diplomacy until I defected to South Korea in the summer of 2016.

But my story is quite different from other defectors who may have experienced political oppression, inhumane treatment in political prison camps, or who left North Korea in order to avoid hunger and economic difficulties.

Rather, today, I would like to tell you about my life as a North Korean diplomat, why I defected to the free world, why Kim Jong-un is developing nuclear and ICBM programs, and how best to deal with the North Korean regime.

I went through elite educational courses in North Korea which could not even be dreamed of by ordinary citizens there. At the age of 14, I was sent to China for a special elite educational program. More than 20 years of my past 55 years of my life were very privileged by North Korean standards. I lived and worked in foreign countries such as China, Denmark, Sweden, and the United Kingdom.

The North Korean system provided me with all kinds of political privileges and economic benefits during this time and in the course of my last posting I was fortunate enough to live in the U.K. with my wife and two sons.

Throughout my life, my family members and relatives were all dedicated true Communists. Ironically, however, I ended up deserting that system and ideology and I am living in South Korea where I do not have any friends or relatives. And today, I am even testifying at the United States Congress, which I had always been taught to fight against.

The reason why I gave up all the privileges and economic benefit was that I felt I could not let my sons lead a life like me as a modern-day slave. I believed the best legacy I could leave for my sons was to give them the freedom that is so common to everyone in America. Had we not defected, I feared that someday my sons would have cursed me for forcing them back to North Korea. They were used to online gaming, Facebook messaging, email, and internet use. I believed my sons would suffer a lot if they returned to the North Korean system.

Indeed, how could any boys raised in the London educational system and familiar with freedom of thought ever go back and reacclimatize to a life in North Korea? I could not confiscate freedom and enjoyment of liberty from them.

I could not take back the happy smiles of my sons by bringing them back to North Korea. I could not force my sons to pretend to be loyal to Kim Jong-un and the North Korean system and to shout, "Long live the Supreme Leader, Kim Jong-un—long live the Socialist paradise of the DPRK," like I did all my life.

As a North Korean diplomat, everyday activities and services were like a leading ceaseless double life, which was psychologically difficult. I have to pretend to be loyal to the Kim Jong-un regime, even though my heart did not agree.

I often was asked questions by my British friends which caught me flat footed, trying to justify the North Korean system when deep down I knew their concerns were fair and legitimate. They asked me things such as, how could Kim Jong-un prosecute his uncle—why does North Korea continue to appeal for humanitarian aid while pouring of millions of dollars into its nuclear and missile development.

Communism has always opposed dynastic transference of power—so how then does the Kim family's hereditary leadership system prevail so long in North Korea? While dealing with these kinds of questions was always painful and they made me increasingly realize the deep-rooted contradictions upon which the entire North Korean system is built.

You might think that living as a member of the elite class in North Korea is all about luxury goods, fine wines, and abuse of power. Yet, the reality for many privileged people in Pyongyang is far different. For example, all high-ranking leaders have to live collectively in separate apartments according to their rank.

Moreover, getting promoted within this system actually requires more sacrifices, reduced freedoms, and an increasing risk of your life, even though you may enjoy more economic benefits as a result.

Indeed, if it is discovered that a senior elite may have different ideas or express private dissatisfactions then he or she could be subject to persecution.

And as you all know, even the members of the Kim's family have been subject to this type of persecution. Such was the case with the killing of Kim Jong-un's uncle, Jang Song-thaek, and half-brother, Kim Jong-nam.

Beyond these high-profile incidents, much more has been going on beneath the surface over the past 5 years. Hundreds of cadres have been persecuted without due process. For example, families of former North Korean Ambassadors to Cuba and Malaysia were sent to prison camps and nobody knows whether they are now alive or dead.

Former North Korean Ambassador to Sweden and the former North Korean Ambassador and Deputy Ambassador to UNESCO were also forced to return back to Pyongyang and expelled from the foreign ministry after the death of Jang Song-thaek.

While on the surface the Kim Jong-un regime seems to have consolidated its power through this reign of terror, simultaneously there are great and unexpected changes taking place within North Korea.

Contrary to the official policy and wishes of the regime, the free markets are flourishing. As more and more people get used to free and capitalistic style markets, the state-owned socialistic economic system becomes increasingly forgotten about.

The welfare system of North Korea has long collapsed and millions of civil servants, army officers, and security forces are dependent on bribes and state asset embezzlement for their survival.

Citizens do not care about state propaganda but increasingly watch illegally imported South Korean movies and dramas. The domestic system of control is weakening as the days go by.

Back in 2010, during the Arab Spring, many experts said that it would be impossible to imagine such similar events taking place in North Korea. These changes, however, make it increasingly possible to think about civilian uprising in North Korea.

As more and more people gradually become informed about the reality of their living conditions, the North Korean Government will either have to change and adapt in positive ways for its citizens or to face the consequences of their escalating dissatisfaction.

Until now, the North Korean system has prevailed through an effective and credible reign of terror and by almost perfectly preventing the free flow of outside information.

Today, Kim Jong-un thinks that only nuclear weapons and ICBMs can help him avoid the continuing disintegration of the North Korean system.

He also thinks that the existence of a prosperous and democratic South Korea so close to the border is by itself a major threat toward his dynasty.

While Kim Jong-un has already long had the tools to destroy South Korea effectively, he also believes it is necessary to drive American forces out of the peninsula, and this can be done, he believes, by being able to credibly threaten the continental United States with nuclear weapons.

On top of thousands of artillery pieces and short-range missile capabilities long held on North Korean side, the potential deployment of battle-ready nuclear ICBMs means the threat is not only toward South Korea but also toward America.

In face of this emerging situation, the U.S. Government is now pursuing a policy of maximum pressure and engagement. However, it will take some time to assess the effectiveness of the current economic sanctions and campaign of diplomatic isolation.

As we wait to see the outcome, we shall seek to continue the momentum and even expand targeted sanctions until the North Korean regime comes back to the dialogue table for denuclearization.

In the face of the emerging threat, we should strengthen the U.S. and Republic of Korea alliance and enhance military preparedness in order to prevent potential nuclear and ICBM provocations by North Korea.

The U.S. and Republic of Korea Governments should enhance the level of their coordination and communication under the slogan of "We go together."

It is a long-established dialogue strategy of North Korea to exclude South Korea while communicating only with the U.S. The United States and South Korean Governments should frustrate this North Korean strategy through strong concerted coordination.

Frankly, Kim Jong-un is not fully aware of the strength and might of American military power. Because of this misunderstanding, Kim Jong-un genuinely believes that he can break the sanctions regime apart once he compels Washington to accept

North Korea's new status after successfully completing the development of his ICBM program and putting the new missiles into deployment.

Some people do not believe in soft power but only in military options. But it is necessary to reconsider whether we have tried all nonmilitary options before we decide that military action against North Korea is all that is left.

Before any military action is taken, I think it is necessary to meet Kim Jong-un at least once to understand his thinking and try to convince him that he would be destroyed if he continues his current direction.

We cannot change the policy of terror of the Kim Jong-un regime but we can educate the North Korean population to stand up by disseminating outside information.

However, is the United States really doing enough in this regard? The U.S. is spending billions of dollars to cope with the military threat and yet how much does the U.S. spend each year on information activities involving North Korea in a year?

Unfortunately, it may be a tiny fraction. Yet, we now know that the communist systems of the Soviet Union and East European countries crumbled as a result of dissemination of outside information and the subsequent changes in thinking caused among people within this systems.

Indeed, the Berlin Wall would not have easily collapsed if East German people did not regularly watch West German TV.

To sum up, much more needs to be done to increase the flow of information into North Korea. German reunification could not have been achieved if the Hungarian Government did not open its border with Austria to provide an exit route for the East German people.

Now some 30,000 North Korea defectors have come to South Korea. In China, however, tens of thousands of North Korean defectors are living without papers under the shadows and are being physically or sexually exploited.

While the U.S. should continue urging China and Russia to support more economic sanctions, it should also do more to stop Beijing repatriating defectors back to North Korea.

The world was united to abolish the South African apartheid. Now it is time for the world to stop the widespread and systematic human rights violations in North Korea, which are tantamount to the crimes committed by the Nazis.

Mr. Chairman, this concludes my opening statement. Thank you again for this opportunity and I look forward to your questions.

[The prepared statement of Mr. Thae follows:]

Testimony of Minister Thae, Yong-ho
House Committee on Foreign Affairs
November 1, 2017

Chairman Royce, Ranking Member Engel, Distinguished Members of the Committee, thank you for the opportunity to be here today.

First, I would like to express my sincere gratitude to Chairman Royce, who kept his promise to accommodate my wishes to visit the United States and gave me this opportunity to testify before the House Committee on Foreign Affairs.

As you are all aware, I worked at the frontline of North Korean diplomacy until I defected to South Korea in 2016. But my story is quite different from other defectors, who may have experienced political oppression, inhuman treatment in political prison camps, or who left North Korea in order to avoid hunger and economic difficulties. Rather, today I would like to tell you about my life as a North Korean diplomat, why I defected to the free world, why Kim Jong Un is developing nuclear and ICBM programs, and how best to deal with the North Korean regime.

I went through elite educational courses in North Korea, which could not even be dreamed of by ordinary citizens there. At the age of 14, I was sent to China for a special elite educational program. More than 20 years of the past 55 years of my life, were very privileged by North Korean standards. I lived and worked in foreign countries such as China, Denmark, Sweden and the United Kingdom. The North Korean system provided me with all kinds of political privileges and economic benefits during this time and, in the course of my last posting, I was fortunate enough to live in the UK with my wife and two sons.

Throughout my life, my family members and relatives were all dedicated true communists. Ironically, however, I ended up deserting that system and ideology, and I am living in South Korea – where I do not have any friends or relatives. And, today, I am even testifying at the United States Congress, which I had always been taught to fight against.

The reason why I gave up all the privileges and economic benefits was that I felt I could not let my sons lead a life like me, as a modern-day slave. I believed the best legacy I could leave for my sons was to give them the freedom that is so common to everyone in America. Had we not defected, I feared that someday my sons would have cursed me for forcing them back to North Korea. They were used to online gaming, Facebook messaging, email and internet news. I believed my sons would suffer a lot if they returned to the North Korean system. Indeed, how could any boys raised in the London education system and familiar with freedom of thought ever go back and re-acclimatize to life in North Korea? I could not confiscate freedom and enjoyment of liberty from them. I could not take back the happy smiles of my sons by bringing them back to North Korea. I could not force my sons to pretend to be loyal to Kim Jong Un and the North Korean system and to shout 'long live the supreme leader Kim Jong Un!,' 'long live the socialist paradise of the DPRK' – like I did all my life.

As a North Korean diplomat, everyday activities and services were like leading a ceaseless double-life, which was psychologically difficult. I had to pretend to be loyal to the Kim Jong Un regime, even though my heart did not agree. I often was asked questions by my British friends which caught me flat footed. Trying to justify the North Korean system when, deep down, I knew their concerns were fair and legitimate. They asked me things such as:

- "How could Kim Jong Un persecute his own uncle?"

- "Why does North Korea continue to appeal for humanitarian aid while pouring hundreds of millions of dollars into its nuclear and missile development?"
- "Communism has always opposed a dynastic transfer of power, so how then does the Kim family's hereditary leadership system prevail so long in North Korea?"

While dealing with these kinds of questions was always painful, they made me increasingly realize the deep-rooted contradictions upon which the entire North Korean system is built.

You might think that living as a member of the elite class in North Korea is all about luxury goods, fine wines and abuse of power. Yet, the reality for many privileged people in Pyongyang is far different. For example, all high-ranking leaders have to live collectively in separated apartments, according to their rank. Moreover, getting promoted within this system actually requires more sacrifices, reduced freedoms and an increasing risk of your life – even though you may enjoy more economic benefits as a result. Indeed, if it is discovered that a senior elite may have different ideas or express private dissatisfactions, then he or she could be subject to persecution. And as you all know, even the members of the Kim's family have been subject to this type of persecution. Such was the case with the killing of Kim Jung Un's uncle Jang Song Thaek and half-brother Kim Jong Nam.

Beyond these high-profile incidents, much more has been going on beneath the surface over the past five years, hundreds of cadres have been persecuted without due process. For example, the families of former North Korean Ambassadors to Cuba and Malaysia were sent to prison camps and nobody knows whether they are now alive or dead. The former North Korean Ambassador to Sweden and the former North Korean Ambassador and deputy Ambassador to UNESCO were also forced to return back to Pyongyang and expelled from the Foreign Ministry after the death of Jang Song Thaek.

While on the surface the Kim Jong Un regime seems to have consolidated its power through this reign of terror, simultaneously there are great and unexpected changes taking place within North Korea. Contrary to the official policy and wish of the regime, the free markets are flourishing. As more and more people get used to free and capitalist-style markets, the state owned socialist economic system becomes increasingly forgotten about. The welfare system of North Korea has long collapsed and millions of civil servants, army officers, and security forces are dependent on bribes and state asset embezzlement for their survival.

The citizens do not care about state propaganda but increasingly watch illegally imported South Korean movies and dramas. The domestic system of control is weakening as the days go by. Back in 2010, during the Arab Spring, many experts said it would be impossible to imagine such similar events taking place in North Korea. These changes, however, make it increasingly possible to think about civilian uprising in North Korea. As more and more people gradually become informed about the reality of their living conditions, the North Korean government will either have to change and adapt in positive ways for its citizens, or to face the consequences of their escalating dissatisfaction. Until now, the North Korean system has prevailed through an effective and credible reign of terror and by almost perfectly preventing the free-flow of outside information.

Today, Kim Jong Un thinks that only nuclear weapons and ICBMs can help him avert the continuing disintegration of the North Korean system. He also thinks that the existence of a prosperous and democratic South Korea so close to the border is, by itself, a major threat towards his dynasty. While Kim Jong Un has already long had the tools to destroy South Korea effectively, he also believes it is necessary to drive American forces out of the peninsula. And this can be done, he believes, by being able to credibly threaten the continental United States with nuclear weapons. On top of the thousands of artillery pieces and short-range missile capabilities long held on the North Korean side, the potential deployment of battle-ready nuclear ICBMs means the threat is not only towards South Korea, but also towards America.

In face of this emerging situation, the U.S. government is now pursuing a policy of 'maximum pressure and engagement'. However, it will take some time to assess the effectiveness of the current economic sanctions and campaign of diplomatic isolation. As we wait to see the outcome, we should seek to continue the momentum and even expand targeted sanctions until the North Korean regime comes back to the dialogue table for denuclearisation.

In face of the emerging threat, we should strengthen the U.S.-ROK alliance and enhance military preparedness in order to prevent potential nuclear and ICBM provocations by North Korea. The US and ROK Governments should enhance the level of their coordination and communication under the slogan of 'We go together.' It is a long established dialogue strategy of North Korea to exclude South Korea while communicating only with the US. The US and South Korean Governments should frustrate this North Korea strategy through strong concerted co-ordination.

Frankly, Kim Jong Un is not fully aware of the strength and might of American military power. Because of this misunderstanding, Kim Jong Un genuinely believes that he can break the sanctions regime apart once he compels Washington to accept North Korea's new status after successfully completing the development of his ICBM program and putting the new missiles into deployment.

Some people do not believe in soft power, but only in military options. But it is necessary to reconsider whether we have tried all non-military options before we decide that military action against North Korea is all that is left. Before any military action is taken, I think it is necessary to meet Kim Jong Un at least once to understand his thinking and to try to convince him that he would be destroyed if he continues his current direction.

We cannot change the policy of terror of the Kim Jong Un regime. But we can educate North Korean population to stand up by disseminating outside information. However, is the United States really doing enough in this regard? The U.S. is spending billions of dollars to cope with the military threat. Yet how much does the U.S. spend each year on information activities involving North Korea in a year? Unfortunately, it may be tiny fraction.

Yet we now know that the communist systems of the Soviet Union and East European countries crumbled as a result of the dissemination of outside information and the subsequent changes in thinking caused among people within those systems. Indeed, the Berlin wall would not have easily collapsed if East German people did not regularly watch West German TV. To sum up, much more needs to be done to increase the flows of information into North Korea. German reunification could not have been achieved if the Hungarian government did not open its border with Austria to provide an exit route for the East German people.

Now some 30,000 North Korea defectors have come to South Korea. In China, however, tens of thousands of North Korean defectors are living without papers, under the shadows, and are being physically or sexually exploited. While the U.S. should continue urging China and Russia to support more economic sanctions, it should also do more to stop Beijing repatriating defectors back to North Korea.

The world was united to abolish the South African apartheid. Now it is time for the world to stop the widespread and systematic human rights violations in North Korea, which are tantamount to the crimes committed by the Nazis.

Mr. Chairman, this concludes my opening statement. Thank you again for this opportunity and I look forward to your questions.

———————

Chairman ROYCE. Thank you very much, Mr. Thae.

You made clear in your remarks that as more and more people gradually become informed about the reality of their living conditions and what they are told is a paradise but they found out how people are living in South Korea or in the rest of the world that North Korea will either have to change and adapt in positive ways for its citizens or to face the consequences of the people's escalating dissatisfaction.

As you said, it has been a powerful impact in Eastern Europe and the Soviet Union and can have the same effect in North Korea. So my question is what kind of messages should we focus on sending into North Korea?

Who are the best? Is it former defectors who have a story to tell, who can report the news of what they have seen in the outside world?

And should our message to, as you said, the elites—should our message to the elites be different than the message that we would help people send to the common people in North Korea?

You have made clear that both are increasingly dissatisfied with the regime. So what would be your suggestion?

Mr. THAE. First, the North Korean system can only be in place by making its leader a god. So we have to find out where is the Achilles heel.

Now, after 5 years in power, Kim Jong-un still cannot tell the North Korean people his date of birth. Nobody in North Korea knows his date of birth.

Nobody in North Korea knows who his mother is. Nobody in North Korea knows his half-brother, Kim Jong-nam. Nobody in North Korea knows that he is the only third son of Kim Jong-il and now Kim Jong-un is brainwashing the North Korean population that he is the only bloodline of Paektu Mountain.

But after 5 years of this kind of continuous brainwashing he still cannot provide the North Korean population with a single photo with his grandfather, Kim Il-sung. Why?

Because he was a hidden boy by his father. He was kept secretly and silently in Switzerland throughout the years. But a majority of the North Korean population do not know this fact.

So we should disseminate the information about him first, who he is—why, even now, Kim Jong-un cannot present even a single photo with his grandfather.

Because his grandfather himself didn't know the existence of this boy. The majority of the North Korean people do not know that his father, Kim Jong-il, had several ladies to live with.

So we should tell the North Korean people that Kim Jong-un and his father, Kim Jong-il and his grandfather, Kim Il-song, the whole member of Kim dynasty are not gods.

That is the first thing we should do and we should disseminate the basic concepts of freedom and human rights. North Korea is a country with a system of classification.

The population of North Korea is divided into different classes and we have to tell the North Korean population how stupid this system is. It is similar to a feudal class system from several hundred years ago.

So we have many things to tell the North Korean people that it is not a paradise. It is not a socialist welfare system. It is the worst inhumane system in human history.

Chairman ROYCE. In terms of our dialogue with Beijing, what should we be pressing Beijing on with respect to North Korea?

Mr. THAE. I think we should continue the current momentum to inducing the Chinese Government to support economic sanctions against North Korea. But that is not enough.

We should urge the Chinese Government not to repatriate North Korean defectors back to North Korea. The Chinese Government knows well that once these defectors are repatriated back to North Korea, they would be the subject of torture.

They would be the subject of enforcement of labor. So we should let the Chinese Government open the route to South Korea for all the hiding North Korean defectors in China.

I mentioned a little bit about the cooperation between the West German Government and Hungarian Government during the process of German reunification.

If the Chinese Government helps North Korean defectors to go freely to South Korea, I think that there could be a massive exodus of North Korean population to China through their borders with China.

Chairman ROYCE. To South Korea through China?

Mr. THAE. Yes, that is right. And if the Chinese open its routes for defectors to South Korea, I think the North Korean system would collapse in a very short span of time.

Chairman ROYCE. Thank you, Mr. Thae.

We go now to Mr. Eliot Engel, our ranking member.

Mr. ENGEL. Thank you, Mr. Chairman.

Mr. Thae, your comments are very riveting, very interesting, and very important to give us an insight.

You know, when I was there, Kim Jong-il was the leader and I know that he was referred to as the Dear Leader and his father was referred to as the Great Leader—Kim Il-song.

I am wondering if Kim Jung-un has a similar title. You walk into every room. There were pictures of the two of them on the wall. It was something very, very scary and eerie. Is that still the case with Kim Jong-un?

Mr. THAE. Of course, and Kim Jong even is upgrading his propaganda campaign to make him appear as a god of the North Korean people.

Mr. ENGEL. Thank you. So let me ask you, is there any scenario you envision in which North Korea might freeze or dismantle its long-range missile or nuclear weapons program? What would be the best means to persuade North Korea to do so?

Mr. THAE. I think, first, Kim Jong-un still believes that he can achieve this goal. So we should continue to tell the North Korean leadership and, if possible, Kim Jong-un himself that America will not accept North Korea as a nuclear-armed state.

North Korea has seen how India and Pakistan achieved that goal and they want to follow the example of India and Pakistan. But we should clarify that this will not be the case for North Korea.

Mr. ENGEL. From what you know about the internal dynamics of the North Korean political and economic systems, how might increased external pressures such as unilateral and multilateral sanctions lead the North Korean Government to change course? Would it? If not, why not?

Mr. THAE. Oh, as I've said, the current economic sanction so far is not enough. So we should increase more targeted sanctions. And second, we have to wait and see the effectiveness of the current economic sanctions.

North Korea is used to that kind of sanctions and North Korea has a certain amount of stockpiles of war. So we have to wait until when North Korea opens its doors for war stockpiles.

When North Korea starts to open its war stockpiles of food and oil, then we may see how long North Korea can sustain.

Mr. ENGEL. Thank you.

You know, one of the things that shocked us when we first came into Pyongyang were these massive billboards—propaganda, political propaganda ones—and one of them had—I don't know if Joe Wilson is here—he was with me.

But he took a picture of one of those posters and it was a North Korean soldier putting a bayonet in the head of an American soldier, and we knew it was an American soldier because his helmet said USA on it.

It was very, very frightening, very scary. And we mentioned it, of course, to all the North Korean authorities. But one thing stuck in my mind.

When we were talking about the nuclear program, one of the higher—we never did meet with the Dear Leader but we met with what I think is the next person whose name I think was also Kim and we were told blankly, and it is the one thing I came home from, they said—he said Saddam Hussein didn't have nuclear weapons and look how he wound up—look what he wound up.

And it really-really showed me a bit of the mind set about how they really think that the nuclear weapons are the key to being players. Otherwise, South Korea would run circles around them because of the prosperity and the economic opportunities and the dynamism of the Seoul regime.

But they, even back then—this was probably about 12 years ago—talked about nuclear weapons as their key to success in the future. Is that still the mind set?

Mr. THAE. Yes. Still the Kim Jong-un regime believes that they can guarantee the permanent system of North Korea by nuclear and ICBM because they think that a prosperous and democratic South Korea itself is threatening the existence of North Korea itself.

That is why they think and believe that ICBM tipped with nuclear weapons in the guarantee for their survival.

Mr. ENGEL. Let me ask you one brief question. My final question is have you observed any changes in North Korea in recent years that might suggest that an expanded United States information campaign targeting audiences inside North Korea might be more successful than past efforts.

How would you go about changing North Korea's perception of the outside world?

Mr. THAE. When the South Korean cultural content first arrived in North Korea through smuggling, North Korean authorities tried every measure to prevent it even by conducting public executions and rampant arrest of the people who watch South Korean movies and dramas.

But whatever measures they take, the demand for South Korean cultural content increased. So the North Korean regime learned that that kind of enforcement cannot solve the problem.

That's why for the past few years they are now developing their own footage to prevent the North Korean population from watching South Korean movies and dramas. How?

They decided to open the film archives of Kim Jong-il and decided to filter for those foreign films from former Soviet Union and former socialist eastern European countries to find out the films which can meet the demand of enjoyment for North Korean people.

So now if you are in the Pyongyang streets there are a lot of stores where they sell those DVD discs with hundreds of Russian films, former East German films, Chinese films and even these days American cartoons like Tom & Jerry, Lion King or Beauty and the Beast, of these even cartoons for the children.

So they learned that in order to fill the demand for outside cultural contents they should do something. So that is why this proved that the North Korean regime is very afraid of dissemination of information.

So I think if we continue to disseminate and if we continue to make tailor-made content for North Korea then I think we can make a change in North Korea.

Up until now, those cultural contents of South Korea which North Korean people are watching are the contents which are produced for South Korean audience, not for North Koreans. So they just watch it for their amusement and entertainment.

But those cultural content so far do not actually relate the North Korean citizens' way of thinking. Those cultural contents cannot make North Koreans critically analyze the life in North Korea.

That's why we should make tailor-made contents which can educate the North Korean population. And I think it is time we should invest to make that kind of very simple tailor-made content which can tell the basic concepts of freedom, human rights, and democracy.

Mr. ENGEL. Thank you very much.

Chairman ROYCE. We go to Mr. Chris Smith of New Jersey.

Mr. SMITH. Thank you so very much. And Mr. Thae, thank you for your courage and for being here providing your insights and observations.

I remember during the worst days of the Cold War it used to be said that the Iron Curtain isn't soundproof, and your idea of really ratcheting up the freedom broadcasting couldn't come at a more timely point in this terrible escalating conflict. So thank you for that, and that has to be followed up on.

Let me ask you two things. First, you've made a stunning observation and recommendation that if China were to receive defectors and facilitate their passage into South Korea that that could truly debilitate this dictatorship and lead to its demise. My question— China, and I've held several hearings on this—China violates the Refugee Convention with impunity.

The whole idea of rapprochement—they send people back who didn't go to the gulag or they benefitted by trafficking those people who come in, particularly the women, into sex trafficking and labor trafficking.

So they are making money out of it and they are also violating the Refugee Convention. My hope is that your words to the Chinese Governments as well as our own Governments will act upon that because that is a very benign and certainly a way of trying to de-escalate and lead to an end to this escalating crisis. So thank you for that. You might want to speak to that further.

Secondly, we underestimate the whole idea of Juche and the cult of personality. Emperor Hirohito and the fanaticism of imperial Japan was based on the belief that he was God and, as you have said, that is exactly how they look at the Kims, particularly Kim Il-sung, and I think there is a gross under appreciation of how that leads to fanaticism and the willingness to die for now the new Kim because he is God.

And I wonder if you could shed some insights into whether or not the people still believe that and to what degree, particularly in the army. We know they have 1 million people active, about 5 million or so ready reserve. I mean, that is a potent force, coupled with nuclear, where they are willing to die for God.

Mr. THAE. First of all, about the defectors' case in China—if you visit the Chinese border with North Korea, you can easily learn that the Chinese Government has built up the extensive network of catching the North Korean defectors along its borders and if a North Korean defector is caught, then he or she could immediately be repatriated.

And if we visit those borders these days, the Chinese have built more fences, more river banks in order to prevent the vast exodus of the North Korean population.

Now the Chinese Government is saying that they are very much concerned of any possible refugee crisis if the North Korean system collapses. But that is not really the truth because North Korean defectors and the North Korean population, they have a place to go once they arrive China.

They have South Korea, which would welcome to accommodate all North Korean defectors from China. So the Chinese argument that they would cover or they would be burdened by all the economic costs of North Korean refugees is not true because there is the Government of South Korea which can accommodate all those North Korean defectors.

So we continue to ask the Chinese Government to open the exit route for North Korean defectors to go to South Korea. We should ask the Chinese Government to establish camps for North Korean defectors for temporary stay and for continuation of their journey to South Korea.

I think that is the thing we should do. And China is the member of Refugee Convention. That's why, as a big country, the Chinese Government has an obligation to observe its international obligation by letting North Korean defectors to go to China.

And the second thing, the personal culture in North Korea, it is really, really surprising because in North Korea when you reach the age of four or five from the age of kindergarten you are brain-washed.

For instance, every morning the young children of 3 or 4 years are forced to bow in front of the portraits of Kim Jong-il, Kim Il-sung, and Kim Jong-un. Then they are offered a cup of milk.

They should stand up and express their thanks before they drink the milk to Kim Jong-un. When there is a harvest of apples, the apples will be distributed to the population as a gift of Kim Jong-un.

So the Kim Jong-un regime established a full scale stupid brain-washing system in order to depict Kim Jong-un as the god.

So I think we should try or concentrate efforts to educate the North Korean people that Kim Jong-un is not a god. He is just a normal human being and the Kim family is not the family of the god.

And we should continue to tell the North Korean people—we should touch the Achilles heel of Kim Jong-un regime. That is my viewpoint.

Mr. SMITH. Thank you.

Chairman ROYCE. Albio Sires of New Jersey is next in the queue.

Mr. SIRES. Thank you, Mr. Chairman.

You know, I am fascinated by your comments but I am not really surprised because I've seen the indoctrination process in other countries and how it works.

I am concerned with the nuclear program. It seems that they have developed this nuclear program very rapidly. Can you talk a little bit about who's assisting them? Because it seems that it is so rapid that somebody had to assist them.

Is it China? Is it Iran? Is it Russia? In your opinion, is anybody involved in assisting with their nuclear proliferation?

Mr. THAE. Oh, it is common knowledge that North Korea's basic knowledge of nuclear weapons all came from the former Soviet Union.

In late of 1960s and the '70s it was the policy of the former Soviet Union to control all the nuclear experts and nuclear industries of former socialist countries by inviting and educating all those nuclear experts in Russia.

So North Korea started to send its young nuclear experts to Russia's nuclear institute from late of 1950s. So, actually, North Korea accumulated the vast knowledge of making these nuclear weapons from Russia.

But, of course, at that time the Soviet Union Government did not intend to tell North Korean nuclear experts how to make nuclear weapons but they educated the North Korean nuclear experts in order to expand their nuclear power industry and in order to control the whole socialist world of nuclear energy.

But the North Korean regime took advantage of this education system built in '50s and '60s and they accumulated the knowledge on how to make it.

But in the past 5 years, we witnessed that there is all of a sudden a kind of quick acceleration of this process of ICBM and nuclear development. So how was it possible?

We learned that in March 2013 the Kim Jong-un regime, the Workers' Party of Korea, adopted a policy of simultaneously developing nuclear weapons and the economy, which is called the Pyongyang policy.

Then what is the difference between Kim Jong-un's policy of nuclear development with his father and with his grandfather? Throughout the history of North Korea, Kim Il-sung and Kim Jong-il never stopped developing nuclear program.

But the main difference between Kim Jong-un and Kim Jong-il is that Kim Jong-un wants to achieve that goal in a very short span of time and in a very open way.

During Kim Jong-il's period, the North Korean regime developed a nuclear program under the pretext of denuclearizing the Korean Peninsula. So in other words, when the Chinese wants to force North Korea to stop it, they always justify to the Chinese Government that, hey, Chinese brother, we need this nuclear weapon in order to lend the ears of Americans.

So our final goal is not the acquisition of nuclear weapons but to reach a kind of deal with Americans. So they cheated the Chinese again and again and again. But these days, no. The justification is different.

North Korea openly stated to China that we want to achieve this goal openly at any cost. And secondly, from March 2013, the North Korean regime decided to invest all available materials and finance for the completion of nuclear weapons.

So that is the main difference between the present North Korean regime and the previous Kim Jong-un's period.

Mr. SIRES. Thank you.

Chairman ROYCE. We go now to Congressman Dana Rohrabacher of California.

Mr. ROHRABACHER. Thank you very much, Mr. Chairman, and thank you very much to our witness today. I appreciate the insights that you are providing us.

A couple of things that you've mentioned I'd like to get some clarification on. Do the people of North Korea know that Kim Jong-un, if I am pronouncing it correctly, was educated in Switzerland and at an elite private school? Do they know that?

Mr. THAE. A majority of the North Korean population didn't know that he was educated in Switzerland. No.

Mr. ROHRABACHER. Don't we have broadcasts going into North Korea? Why would the people of North Korea not know that what he is doing to them he was spared and that he lived in a totally different life than what they are expected to live? Are broadcasts not being aggressive enough if the people of North Korea don't know that?

Mr. THAE. Oh, but maybe about those—you know, the balloons of the pamphlets or the numbers of the radios have reached inside of North Korea in secret ways.

But so far, the effect of that kind of devices is not very efficient. So I think in order to vastly disseminate the information to the North Korean people I think we should develop new ways to do it.

For instance, one thing I have in mind is that now we can have a kind of satellite TV transmissions for North Korean people and we can smuggle in the small devices like DMB things which is the similar size of smart phone or radio so let the North Koreans watch the South Korean and American TV networks through that kind of device by the transmission from satellite.

Mr. ROHRABACHER. That sounds like a—frankly, that sounds like an effective use of money as compared to some of the other things that we are doing to try to deal with this threat because if we do not deal with this threat we are putting not only the people of South Korea but putting the American people in severe jeopardy here—in danger.

Let me ask—you mentioned—how is religion treated in North Korea?

Mr. THAE. Oh, the North Korea system is based on contradictions. For instance, the North Korean constitution allows the freedom of belief.

But in North Korean society where the constitution does not prevail. The charter of the Workers' Party of Korea and the teachings by Kim Jong-un prevails over the constitution.

So if you read the charter of Workers' Party of Korea and the teachings of Kim Jong-un and the works of Kim Il-sung and Kim Jong-il, it clarified very clearly that two-tier ideology and Kim Il-sung and Kim Jong-ilism should be the only idea of North Korean society.

Mr. ROHRABACHER. Do they permit people to go to church?

Mr. THAE. There are a few churches only in Pyongyang just for show for foreign audiences, not for North Korean people.

Mr. ROHRABACHER. Do the North Korean people have, as I have understood has happened in China in the beginning, worship services in their homes?

Do they get together and pray and is there a religious movement in—South Korea has a tremendous expansion of faith and is that anywhere experienced in North Korea?

Mr. THAE. If that kind of practice is detected by the regime, then it could be the imminent subject of persecution or public execution. That is why I don't think that the people would gather for that kind of the religious practice. But I am not quite sure whether there are individuals who do that kind of belief practices secretly inside their homes. But in my life, I haven't seen that kind of secret practice of religious belief.

Mr. ROHRABACHER. Well, we need to be the champion of these oppressed people around the world, especially when it comes to Christians who are oppressed like this because our own national security will be enhanced by that.

So doing what's right by religious people being persecuted for their religion can probably help us, and thank you very much for sharing your insights with us today.

Mr. THAE. Thank you.

Chairman ROYCE. Representative Bill Keating of Massachusetts.

Mr. KEATING. Thank you, Mr. Chair. And Mr. Thae, thank you very much for your desire and courage to be here.

Just this morning I was at a breakfast of experts discussing North Korea's threat to us as well as their rationale for many of their activities.

They suggested that their ICBM and their nuclear development was to preserve the regime from international threats but also they said it is there for domestic support as well.

And you had said there is an escalating dissatisfaction among the people. So could you explain their rationale and saying is there a group that sees support of the regime because of that nuclear development?

Mr. THAE. I don't understand your last question. What was it?

Mr. KEATING. That Kim Jong-un is developing nuclear weapons and ICBMs just to gather support and stability in his regime in his country, within it.

You said that it is de-escalating, his support. So what is the rationale as other people that see that development as stabilizing and give the regime support as a result?

Mr. THAE. Yes. The first, Kim Jong-un is very well aware that the North Korean system is in the process of disintegration. That is why he looked for any solution to do it and he believes that a ICBM tipped with nuclear weapons can provide him a kind of legitimacy of the leadership for next several decades. Why? Yes——

Mr. KEATING. So the people inside feel that this will help them from an outside threat, as they perceive it. Is that correct?

Mr. THAE. Both ways. Kim Jong-un thinks that with the nuclear weapons he can guarantee the sustainability of his rule.

And the second thing is that in order to get the legitimacy of long-term leadership, something that he wants to convince the whole North Korean elite and the people that he is the one who made North Korea a nuclear power and he wants to convince the North Korean population that once he acquired these nuclear weapons he can easily break the sanctions scheme with America.

Mr. KEATING. Okay. Thank you very much. That's the rationale. This is a really tough question I am going to ask you, one we should all be asking, frankly, because there is a great deal of discussion, even this morning, that there is indeed a likelihood of military intervention preemptively by the U.S. as a defense.

And here is my question: What's going to happen when the missiles stop? What's the next day going to be like? Who is going to be in charge? How are we going to keep stability?

What is China going to do? What are we going to do with the human impact of that as well? As someone that has been in Europe, will our partners be on board? What are your thinkings on this very important issue?

Mr. THAE. After Kim Jong-un finishes his completion of nuclear weapons, then he wants to open a dialogue and deal with America.

He would continue to blackmail America with a possible nuclear war with America and may ask America to pull American forces from South Korea.

Mr. KEATING. Right. I apologize. But what would happen—here is the scenario, that if we did that——

Chairman ROYCE. If I could just interrupt for a minute. He has a follow-up point that he wants to make about what—I think about what would happen next to South Korea if that happens. Then we will continue with your question.

Mr. KEATING. Oh, if I could give him time to answer that. Thank you.

Mr. THAE. Yes. So what he thinks—what his roadmap and strategy is like this. Once he has this nuclear weapon and ICBM, he wants to make a deal with the Americans by asking for scaled-down joint military exercises against North Korea and, finally, pull American forces out from the Korean Peninsula.

If America does not accept his offer, then he may continue to blackmail, like, another test fire or ICBM or something like that so that it will compel Washington to accept his demands.

And Kim Jong-un thinks that if American forces are out of the Korean Peninsula, the next day the foreign investment would follow the American forces, and then when the foreign investments are out of South Korea then the elite and the companies of South Korea would follow the exit.

So he thinks that he can create a kind of massive exodus in South Korean system if he has these nuclear weapons. That is what North Korean regime learned from the case of South Vietnam, when America pulled its troops out from South Vietnam in 1974.

At that time, I think we should remember that the army of South Vietnam was number four in military terms. But when America pulled its forces from South Vietnam, later the foreign investments left. When foreign investments left South Vietnam then the elite of South Vietnam ruling class started to flee. So within 2 years, within 2 years in South Vietnam there was a kind of huge trend of fleeing.

So North Vietnam waited for 2 years and then started an offensive in 1976 and all of a sudden the huge military establishment of South Vietnam was useless to defend its system.

So the North Korean regime learned all these processes. That's why they want to follow the same suit on South Korea. That's why with that ICBM they want to change the current tide of struggle between North Korea and South Korea.

Mr. KEATING. Wow. Thank you. I yield back.

Chairman ROYCE. Mr. Mike McCaul of Texas.

Mr. McCAUL. Thank you, Mr. Chairman.

I think this is one of the most complex challenging foreign policy issues of our time and whenever a power becomes a nuclear power you can't take it away from them.

And we saw that happen in Pakistan in the A.Q. Khan network proliferating to Iran, North Korea. I think this is the result of a policy of neglect in prior administrations, both Republican and Democrat, not dealing with North Korea and now we are in a situation where we are today where I don't see a whole lot of good options on the table.

It is a fact that he has this ICBM capability, that he's miniaturized the nuclear warheads. By all accounts, the IC, while maybe not definitive, we think he may have that capability now as well.

And I talked to the Ambassador from Japan the other day and they are terrified of the prospects. I don't know now to get rid of this guy, and we talk about regime change. We talk about opening channels, letting people defect and a lot of different things.

We know China is the strongest country to deal with North Korea and it is in their best interest, in their back yard. And yet, we are seeing satellite photographs after the U.N. sanctions was voted defying those sanctions with boats going back and forth between China and North Korea.

So that hasn't had a whole lot of impact. So, you know, it has been very interesting. I mean, let me commend you for your courage coming here today in light of the dangers and the obvious risks that you're taking. I think you're a courageous individual.

But they are almost deified, this dynasty. So I don't—I just—how do we change that? First question.

Second one is if the military option is on the table and Secretary Mattis has warned against it, but if that happened what would the Peninsula look like? What would be the aftermath of the military option?

Mr. THAE. The first, I think many people do not understand why the North Korean regime believes that nuclear weapons can solve their problems and why Kim Jong-un's regime is so much obsessed with this kind of nuclear weapons program, which can do nothing but all those, you know, sanctions or whatever.

But from the perspective of the North Korean regime and the Kim Jong-un regime, so far they really believe in this kind of goal can be achieved.

So for instance, now let's review about a U.S. and R.O.K. military alliance. Let's compare the military alliance between South Korea and America and a military alliance between China and North Korea.

The North Korean regime learned that there are a lot of loopholes in the military alliance between South Korea and America. For instance, in that military alliance treaty there is not any clause of compulsory involvement in military alliance with South Korea.

So if a state of war or any kind of war happens on the Korean Peninsula, both sides would discuss. That is the clause. There is nothing legally binding.

But if you read the North Korean military alliance with China, there is a compulsory clause. If war happens on Korean Peninsula, then Chinese side will automatically naturally be involved in this war.

And secondly, if we see the military alliance treaty between South Korea and America, there is a kind of very loose clause how this treaty goes on and how this treaty breaks down.

If one party of this treaty says goodbye 1 year in advance, then this military alliance would disappear. That is the present reality. But if we read the North Korean military alliance with China, it is a kind of divorce agreement.

If one of the parties do not agree to break this treaty, then this treaty would last again and again and again. So I think we have to cover up all those loopholes in military alliance between R.O.K. and America.

That is why North Koreans still believe that if they have these nuclear weapons and continue to blackmail and it can make the strategists in Washington to think whether America is ready to sacrifice their citizens in return for protecting the whole South Korea territory and it strongly believes to do that because they learned from the history about the lessons of Acheson line.

In January 1950, then the Secretary of State, Acheson, drew that Acheson line. Actually, that is the line of defense between South Korea and Japan. So at that time, America did not include South Korea as their own sphere of protection.

That prompted the decision of Korean War by Stalin and Kim Il-sung? Why? Because Soviet Union succeeded in nuclear tests in August 1949 and after the success of nuclear tests by Soviet Union the strategists in Washington thought how to prevent any kind of accidental nuclear war with the Soviet Union.

So they decided to draw a line of defense and unfortunately, they drew that red line not on 38th Parallel but the place on the sea between South Korea and Japan. So from these precedents of Vietnam case, Korean War case, even Chinese case, because the Chinese Communist Party also succeeded in driving American forces out from Taiwan in 1979 by completing its ICBM program.

So from these precedents in history, North Korean communists learned that once they acquired this technology and means to attack America and if they continue to blackmail until America and Washington accepts their deal, they can prevail in this game. That is their strong belief.

And the second thing about the military, the option, of course, I strongly believe that if there is any preventive or surgical strike or whatever, I think the war will be won by America and South Korea.

There is no doubt about it. But we have to see the human sacrifice from this military option. Now there are tens of thousands of North Korean artilleries and short-range missiles are ready to fire at any moment along the military demarcation line and North Korean officers are trained to press the button without any further instructions from the general command if something happens on their side.

So if there is any sound of fire or bomb or strike from Americans, the military artilleries and short-range missiles will fire against South Korea. And we have to remember that tens of millions of South Korean populations are living 70 to 80 kilometers away from this military demarcation line, a very short distance of range of fire—and nobody can calculate but I think certain human sacrifice would happen because of this military option.

So as I've said, there are tremendous changes that are taking place inside North Korea in spite of this reign of terror by the Kim Jong-un regime. If we are determined to use and expand our soft power, I think one day we can reach the same goal we achieved with the former Soviet Union and those former East European socialist countries.

Mr. McCAUL. Very insightful. Thank you.

Chairman ROYCE. Representative Tulsi Gabbard of Hawaii.

Ms. GABBARD. Thank you, Mr. Chairman.

Thank you very much for your courage and your openness and being here to share your story and experience not only with us but with everyone who is watching this.

To follow up on your last statement, so what you are saying is that if there is even a very limited preemptive military strike from the United States that this automatic response using the artillery and short-range missiles would occur. Is that right?

Mr. THAE. Yes, that is right.

Ms. GABBARD. You spoke earlier in your testimony about exhausting all diplomatic measures before turning toward military action and you mentioned about the need to meet with Kim Jong-un directly.

Mr. THAE. Yes. That is right.

Ms. GABBARD. What would need to happen in that conversation to create even just the beginnings of a process that would result ultimately in dismantling and denuclearization of the Peninsula? And how would that be different from previous failed efforts in the past?

Mr. THAE. Oh, I think, first of all, we should tell Kim Jong-un that the North Korean nuclear case is quite different from India, Pakistan, or China because India and Pakistan achieved their goal without making any enemies with the big powers like America, China, or Russia.

So that is why in reality there was not big country who was so serious to stop the nuclear arming in India and Pakistan. But the North Korea case is different because North Korea wants to achieve that goal by blackmailing, by threatening America's interests and the American continent.

So that is the great difference, though. So we should tell Kim Jong-un that his goal to achieve the nuclear status cannot be achievable because as long as America will not accept North Korea as a nuclear state forever.

We have to tell him correctly, and we should tell Kim Jong-un that America is ready to use all military options if Kim Jong-un continues this process and we should tell Kim Jong-un that if Kim Jong-un stops this process and gives up his ambition of ICBM and nuclear development, America is ready to help Kim Jong-un to build his economy and to make North Korea a prosperous country. I think that is the point we should directly deliver to Kim Jong-un.

Ms. GABBARD. You know, it has been spoken about how one of the major reasons why Kim Jong-un is holding and tightening his grip on these nuclear weapons is as a deterrent against any attempts by the United States or others to topple him and his regime, thinking that this will be the only thing that will protect him.

Why is it that if the United States sits down directly with Kim Jong-un that you think he will react positively to a message of we will help you—make sure that your people and your economy prosper? That doesn't appear to seem something that he's been concerned about in the past.

Mr. THAE. Oh, as I've said that Kim Jong-un and the North Korean regime believes that their rival is South Korea, is the biggest threat to the North Korean system itself because Kim Jong-un is very aware that the North Korean population are watching South Korean movies and dramas.

He knows that the minds of North Koreans are changing toward South Korea. So he needs a kind of permanent guarantee to protect his dynasty from that kind of gain and he strongly believes that nuclear weapons can be used as a kind of very strong defense of his dynasty.

So I think we should tell Kim Jong-un that this cannot be the effective way for his sustainability of his leadership and rule in North Korea.

Ms. GABBARD. And you've talked about a little bit of a change in the current in the feeling of the North Korean people. Given the threats upon anyone who expresses even a little bit of dissent or disagreement, do you think Kim Jong-un or his regime is even aware of this change in currents of the North Korean people?

Mr. THAE. Yes, he's very well aware of that because he has a very good network of reporting of the happenings inside of North Korea and so far the Kim Jong-un regime has taken huge measures to prevent the North Korean population from watching South Korean movies and dramas.

But it turned out to be a failure, and also they threw out the system of free market. The North Korean regime tried to prevent the escalation of a free market system in North Korea but failed. So now North Korea is at the stage of more or less accepting this trend of the free marketization process in North Korea.

So they know quite well of this disintegrating process.

Chairman ROYCE. We need to go to General Scott Perry of Pennsylvania.

Mr. PERRY. Thank you, Mr. Chairman.

And Mr. Thae, we are impressed by your courage and we are privileged to have you here today.

Would there be any effect at all on North Korea being named a state sponsor of terror once again? Would that have any effect whatsoever to the regime or their actions?

Mr. THAE. I think that that can be very helpful because once North Korea is reregistered as the state sponsor of terrorism, it can be easier to drive North Korea from all international financial systems and we can also convince the other partners of the world to detect or stop all those—the channels North Korea uses these days to fund their nuclear development.

Mr. PERRY. It seems to me that a big part of our strategy should be and is the relationship with China and North Korea. But it also seems to me that China isn't forthcoming with their agreements.

They water down the agreements. They don't follow the agreements that they have. Is China really the lynchpin that we think it is? Is it the center of gravity? Can they make the difference?

If they stop—where China is—90 percent of North Korea's trade is with China. You know, coal alone $1 billion annually. If China would live up to its agreements can it have the effect that we hope it would with North Korea? Can it bring Kim Jong-un; not the people, unfortunately, but can it bring the regime to its knees?

Mr. THAE. First of all, I would like to avail this opportunity to tell you that during the Trump administration's short span of time America has made a great success in convincing Chinese to take more sanctions against North Korea.

But meanwhile, we should continue to ask the Chinese to stop and crack down on all those smuggling networks between North Korea and China because if the Chinese Government officially limits the trade with North Korea it can easily produce another negative effect by more smugglings between China and North Korea because along the border line between China and North Korea there are hundreds of private traders, small companies who are smuggling and who are involved with dealing these illicit activities with North Korea.

And so far, the Chinese Government has been reluctant to crack down all these other smuggling networks between China and North Korea.

So I think it is time you should raise the issue of this smuggle with the Chinese Government and if Chinese Government further upgrades the level of sanctions I think it will create a big pain on the Kim Jong-un regime.

Mr. PERRY. Could that Chinese smuggling be used to our advantage regarding the information flow into North Korea? There is one thing to get the information there whether you broadcast, whether you somehow smuggle it in, DVDs, thumb drives, what have you, but I also wonder about the other side of that equation, the North Korean people's ability to access it. Is that a possibility, since you mentioned it?

Mr. THAE. Oh, it has two aspects. For instance, I think if the possibility of smuggling is expanded there can be more opportunity of smuggling these devices into North Korea.

But on the other end, if the smuggling opportunity is expanded I think the North Korean regime will be able to import what they wanted.

But the materials which the North Korea regime wants to import are big things like oil or those special—the metals or engines for their military and equipment.

But the things we want to disseminate is the very small things. For instance, due to the recent development of ideology, the technology, the devices of these for dissemination is getting smaller and smaller.

For instance, 5 years ago, if you want to disseminate the contents, you should make this size of DVD and this size of USB stick.

But nowadays, those devices become smaller, around this size of a small SD card. So in North Korea, young children call this SD card, nose card, because why they call it nose card? If their bodies are searched, they can easily put that card inside their nose to avoid searching.

Mr. PERRY. Mr. Thae, may I ask you one question, one more question in the short amount of time I have left? Since I've been a little boy, I've heard about American prisoners from Vietnam and the Second World War being held in POW camps in North Korea.

Is there any truth of that, to your knowledge? Would you have any knowledge of that? Was it ever discussed? What do you know about that, if anything?

Mr. THAE. Oh, to be honest, I have no idea about it.

Mr. PERRY. Thank you, Mr. Ambassador.

Chairman ROYCE. We go now to Representative Norma Torres from California.

Ms. TORRES. Thank you, Mr. Chairman.

Mr. Thae, thank you for joining us today. I am trying to comprehend what caused you and the wave of defectors to leave during the time that you left versus under the previous Supreme Leader. Can you talk a little bit about that?

Mr. THAE. You mean my case?

Ms. TORRES. Mm-hmm.

Mr. THAE. Oh, first of all, I would like to tell the members here that I am not the only North Korean diplomat who defected in——

Ms. TORRES. It was a wave. Right.

Mr. THAE. There are more North Korean defectors who—I mean, diplomats who defected. But this is the matter of whether they are willing to open their identity or not. But, you know, as I have told you that I was fortunate to bring my wife and two sons here in——

Ms. TORRES. We have very limited time, sir.

Mr. THAE. Yes. Yes.

Ms. TORRES. I apologize.

Mr. THAE. That's right. So but out of my colleagues who are also diplomats, they have their, you know, their siblings and——

Ms. TORRES. Why now and not before, sir?

Mr. THAE. Yes. So actually the number of diplomat defections is more than we estimate.

Ms. TORRES. More now or more under the previous——

Mr. THAE. Under previous—yes, I meant in the past 2 or 3 years.

Ms. TORRES. 2 or 3 years under——

Mr. THAE. Kim Jong-un regime.

Ms. TORRES. Right.

Mr. THAE. Yes.

Ms. TORRES. Why now under this regime and not the previous? What's the difference? What caused you to say enough is enough?

Mr. THAE. Because the first Kim Jong-un escalated his reign of terror of this kind of thing. So many diplomats and elite group lost confidence on the system and also now Kim Jong-un is desperately accelerating this nuclear process which is very, very dangerous to the existence of North Korea.

Ms. TORRES. Was there something specific to you personally that caused you to say this is it, it's time for me to leave?

Mr. THAE. Oh, there is not that kind of, you know, triggering point. But as I have said that I have watched and followed those growing process of my sons in London and I thought that it is not the right thing for me to take them back.

Ms. TORRES. Mr. Kim Jong-un is a young man. He's going to have a birthday on January 8th.

Mr. THAE. That's right. But nobody knows which year.

Ms. TORRES. Between Russia and China, who do you think is more involved in advising him on issues dealing with the U.S.?

Mr. THAE. I don't think China or Russia is advising Kim Jong-un on that matter. He is advised by his close associates.

Ms. TORRES. Yet, China is very dependent on workers from North Korea.

Mr. THAE. Yes.

Ms. TORRES. So how can it be that China is not advising him on how to deal with the U.S.?

Mr. THAE. Oh, I mean that I don't think that the Chinese has any kind of, you know, the diplomatic instrument which can change the thought of Kim Jong-un and also it is a common fact that China is exercising the double standard—the approach on North Korea on one hand.

China is keeping its obligation with United Nations sanctions but on the other hand it is also opening the possibilities for North Korea to fund its program by importing a lot of North Korean laborers to their country.

Ms. TORRES. Smuggling networks, private traders, small companies, do you have an idea of, you know, who they are and how we can as a U.S. policy impact that activity?

Mr. THAE. I think that is the matter of the Chinese decision. I think we should continue to convince the Chinese Government that the North Korean nuclear threat is not only a threat to America but it can be the threat to China itself.

So I think we should continue to convince the Chinese Government to cooperate to stop North Korea's nuclearization and if the Chinese are convinced then I think the Chinese Government will take effective measures to stop and crack down all the smuggling networks.

Ms. TORRES. So what I am understanding——

Chairman ROYCE. Okay. Well, the time has expired, though.

Ms. TORRES. Thank you. I yield back.

Chairman ROYCE. Okay. We have got to go to Joe Wilson of South Carolina.

Mr. WILSON. Thank you, Mr. Chairman.

And Ambassador Thae, I appreciate your courage on behalf of the Korean people. I represent many constituents in South Carolina who have served in Korea.

They developed a great affection for Korean families. I can identify because my dad served in the Flying Tigers to World War II and he developed a great affection for the people of India and China.

Additionally, I want you to know that the Korean-American population is so important across the United States but in my home state of South Carolina this weekend we had the Korean festival and it is to celebrate the extraordinary culture of Korea.

And at Columbia, South Carolina, the Korean Presbyterian Church led by Reverend Dong-young Kim, there will be a great celebration of how much the people of America appreciate the culture of Korea.

And Mr. Chairman, I appreciate your leadership promoting freedom for the Korean citizens, which is of the utmost importance for the people of South Korea and American families for our security.

It is for this reason I'd like to thank the chairman for his attention to a bill that has been proposed by Congressman Adam Schiff of California.

It's a bipartisan bill that supports and clarifies and compliments the State Department's recent prohibition on the tourist travel in North Korea, sadly reflecting on the murder of Otto Warmbier.

Mr. Thae, would you agree that, sadly, North Korea is a supremely dangerous place? And I applaud the State Department with the leadership of President Donald Trump and U.N. Ambassador Nikki Haley for their efforts, through the expeditious passage of the H.R. 2397, the North Korea Travel Control Act.

The danger that North Korea poses to America and our allies is a bipartisan concern and I am just so grateful that both Chairman Ed Royce and Ranking Member Eliot Engel have supported its passage out of the Subcommittee on Asia and the Pacific.

And Ambassador Thae, I have recently visited the beautiful country of South Korea. What an extraordinary country, and I know the critical relationship that we have that "we go together."

Additionally, I am grateful that with Chairman Royce and Congressman Eliot Engel we are possibly the only Members of Congress who have been to North Korea.

We saw the destitution, oppression of the people in Pyongyang but that is in contrast to the extraordinary success of the people of South Korea, the Republic of Korea, and in Seoul.

With that in mind, there have been measures passed both in Congress and at the U.N., led by Ambassador Nikki Haley—the former governor of my home state, South Carolina—that targeted North Korean textiles, coal, iron ore, seafood, and other sectors that are used to finance the illicit programs of the North Korean regime.

Are there any other sectors or streams of revenue that we could act? I am also grateful that President Donald Trump has begun a process of what's called secondary sanctions. Can you suggest to the President any secondary sanctions that should be enforced to help the people of Korea?

Mr. THAE. Oh, I think they could target the measures taken by something like a secondary boycott. I strongly believe that these kind of secondary boycott measures should be expanded to target the Chinese and Russian companies who helps the illicit activity by North Korea.

But meanwhile, I also want to use diplomatic soft power, something like a campaign to isolate North Korea and in diplomatic world.

Ironically, so far only a few countries in the world expelled North Korean Ambassadors as a protest of the current continuation of nuclear program.

For instance, now North Korea has conducted six nuclear tests. But except Spain, no European countries so far have ever expelled or downgraded the current diplomatic relations with North Korea.

What happened between Iran and European countries in the past because of the case of Rashid, the Iranian novelist, at that time the whole European Union, together with America, joined in their efforts to isolate Iran diplomatically by withdrawing all the Ambassadors from Tehran and asking Iran to withdraw their Ambassadors from all European capitals. But so far, we haven't seen that kind of concerted or unified response from Western European countries which we share common ideas and values.

So that is why I think the American Government should beef up more its campaign of diplomatic isolation against North Korea, asking the American allies to follow the suit, to follow the America's policy to isolate North Korea diplomatically.

Now, North Korean workers—tens of thousands of North Korean workers are working in American Middle East allies like Kuwait, the Arab Emirates. But these Arab countries are still allowing North Korean workers working in their countries.

American allies like Poland are still allowing the North Korean workers working in their shipyards. So a lot of measures can be taken with the cooperation with American allies. Why can't the American Government ask Arab allies to do more?

Chairman ROYCE. And if I could interrupt at that point. We have passed sanctions legislation which allows us to deploy sanctions against those entities and we should be doing that. It's a very good point.

We need to go to Mr. Brad Schneider of Illinois.

Mr. WILSON. Ambassador, you're an inspiration. So is our chairman. Thank you.

Chairman ROYCE. Mr. Brad Schneider of Illinois.

Mr. SCHNEIDER. Thank you, Mr. Chairman, and thank you for providing this opportunity for Mr. Thae to join us.

It was an honor to be with the chairman in South Korea in August and a chance to meet with you there. I thank you for that time. I appreciate you coming here and sharing your experiences, your insights. It's very important that you're here and your candor and frankness is very much appreciated.

One of the things you mentioned is that as the elite within North Korea get promoted, it involves greater sacrifice and entails increasing risk.

Given that, what would be the impact in North Korea of providing more opportunities for the elite to defect and how might the international community go to creating those opportunities for defection?

Mr. THAE. Yes. I think we should have a tailor-made system for North Korean elites to defect. For instance, before I defected to South Korea, I studied about the system of South Korea what can I do—what kind of life in my future in South Korea.

I searched all the contents on the Internet. But before my arrival to South Korea and spent a few months in South Korea, I could not get any informations what kind of treatment or what kind of status I can be given by the South Korean Government.

But, of course, the policy of equal treatment for North Korean defectors in South Korea. But as for high elite defectors, I think we should make a tailor-made law so that if we make the exit of North Korean elites for defection I think we should upgrade more the current treatment the policies of North Korea's elite group because the country, like North Korea, can be easily collapsed if the group of elite leave that system.

Mr. SCHNEIDER. Great. Thank you.

I liked how you described the thumb drives that are now nose drives that young people can hide. But that is just a mechanism to get more information into the mass population of North Korea.

I know others have touched on it a little bit but could you expand a bit about some of the most important messages we need to communicate to the people of North Korea to try to unravel the brainwashing that is coming from the Kim regime and expose North Koreans to what is the reality within their country but also the reality in South Korea and the rest of the world.

Mr. THAE. I think we can make tailor-made contents comparing the reality in North Korea and South Korea because North and South, we share the same language, same culture, and also we have huge separate families who also have bloodlines.

That's why I think if we make good tailor-made contents to educate the North Korean people, something like we may use the ordinary daily life of North Koreans. For instance, in North Korea there is no concept of a proper payment for the labor they sacrificed.

North Korea was in place for several decades without proper payment. For instance, when I worked as the deputy general director of North Korea's foreign ministry, my monthly salary was $2,900 North Korean won.

At that time, one kilo of rice was $3,400 won. So with 1 month's salary, I cannot even afford to buy one kilo of rice. So the North Korean system is kind of stupid but people just take it for granted because they are used to this kind of stupidity for a long time and nobody thinks it is strange.

So that is why we should educate the North Korean people that everyone in the North Korean system are entitled for proper payment.

Mr. SCHNEIDER. In your sense and your experience, is this something that should be done in high production qualities or is it more important that it is coming from people—as you mentioned, there were the connections—familiar connections, North Koreans and South Koreans share those bonds—is it something that should be done showing every—just everyday life in South Korea?

Mr. THAE. No, every life in North Korea, I mean.

Mr. SCHNEIDER. Right. But showing to the North Koreans what it is like, everyday life in South Korea—that there is opportunity, that someone gets a fair day's wage for a fair day's work—that there is opportunity to raise your family and give them a better future than what their parents are enduring right now?

Mr. THAE. Yes, something like that. For instance, yesterday I told a very interesting story at CSIS about the cultural concepts in North Korea.

In North Korea, for instance, when the girls with physical beauty reaches the age of 14, they are automatically and naturally registered by the regime. And when the girls reach the age of 16 and 17 and if they—the girls keep that physical beauty then they would be mobilized to be sent to the capital to be employed either in special hospitals or guest houses for the entertainment of the Kim family.

But in North Korea, if the young girl with physical beauty is sent to Pyongyang for that purpose, the villagers of that village would regard it as a kind of honor of the family.

It is really a stupid culture which was practiced and prevailed, say, for hundreds of years ago in Yi Dynasty of Korea. But still the North Korean people believe that they—the Kim family can exploit sexually their daughters—you know, beautiful daughters.

So it is really stupid, the system and culture. We should educate the North Korean people how stupid they are by sending their beautiful daughters to the capital.

Mr. SCHNEIDER. Okay. Well, I am out of time. Thank you.

Chairman ROYCE. We need to now—yes. We need to now go to Brian Mast from Florida. Major?

Mr. MAST. Thank you, Chairman, and thank you, sir, for your remarks today. You have spoken a little bit about the history of nuclear development in North Korea.

I believe you were speaking about the Joint Institute for Nuclear Research previously—that overlap between Russia and North Korea, going back quite a long way. And we are all very familiar with the proliferation efforts of A.Q. Khan.

I want to ask a little bit more modernly to your knowledge. Has there been any effort by China to share either nuclear technology or ballistic missile technology with North Korea in modern history?

Mr. THAE. Oh, first of all, I do not have any clear information in fact of this nuclear cooperation between North and China.

But it is a common fact that all those—the ferries which carry all those—the trucks which carry the ICBMs are Chinese-made trucks. This is a very common thing. Even though China claims that those trucks were exported to North Korea for the timber industry but it is a proven fact that North Korea is actually using all those China-made trucks for ICBM deployment.

So and another thing—it is true that in '60s and '70s the basic technology of North Korean submarines were imported from China and hundreds of Chinese technicians helped North Korea to build the first class of submarines.

Mr. MAST. I do want to get to submarines in a moment. That is part of, you know, the whole idea of nuclear triad. Before I ask that question, though, to your knowledge has North Korea had a desire to or actually engaged in sharing their advancements with Iran?

Mr. THAE. Oh, in the past, whenever North Korea test those satellites, Iranian scientists were invited to the site and it is the common fact that during the war between Iraq and Iran, North Korea supported the Iran side by supplying vast—the military equipments and after that ended, because of that there was strong cooperation between Iran and North Korea on all military terms.

But in terms of nuclear cooperation, I do not have any clear fact information of that in that regard.

Mr. MAST. North Korea is not a member of the Nuclear Non-Proliferation Treaty. It's known that they pulled out in 2003. In your opinion, would they share their advancements in nuclear technology with Iran? Do you think that they would have a desire to do that?

Mr. THAE. Absolutely, because North Korea is a country who wants to sell anything for hard currency. It has proved on a couple of occasions that North Korea was engaged in illicit activities like counterfeiting currencies, drugs. So why not their nuclear technology?

Mr. MAST. So you did bring up submarines and there is quite often the emphasis and conversation is placed on ICBM technology.

I would like to know, from your knowledge, has there been an effort to advance capabilities that would allow delivery of a nuclear weapon from a submarine system where they could get off the coast of Japan or South Korea or the United States or any other area of the coast? Has there been a desire or an effort to advance in their submarine delivery capabilities?

Mr. THAE. Oh, it was reported a couple of times and North Korea also claimed that it made dramatic improvements in their submarine delivery especially by—in terms of code launching the technology.

And last year, North Korea proved a couple of times that it made great advancements in SLMB, the test and I am sure that North Korea will continue on that process.

Mr. MAST. I have one final question as it pertains to, I guess the best way I could put it, would be safety. You know, historically speaking, in the world of nuclear weapons between the United States of America and Russia there have been very known protocols.

At one point, it was mutually assured destruction and then there was a ladder of escalation—that everybody knew what the various steps of that were—you know, selective ambiguity.

And so what I would like to know is has North Korea, in an effort to obtain a nuclear weapon, have they also made an effort to secure any of the safety protocols that have existed with the United States of America or Russia to ensure that there is not an accidental launch of a weapon or that somebody that is not part of the regime in control could get in control of a nuclear football, as we call it here, and make a launch? Has there ever been any safety efforts?

Mr. THAE. Oh, last year North Korea announced that the North Korean army's strategic military unit, which means the ICBM missile unit, directly belongs to Kim Jong-un himself. They officially announced it.

So this means that Kim Jong-un wants to delegate the direct instructions from his command directly to the general who is in charge of that whole missile unit.

And I haven't read or seen any of that kind of safety—the regulations how to control or manage North Korea's nuclear arsenal. Personally, I haven't heard any of that kind of the regulations or procedures.

Chairman ROYCE. We need to go to Colonel Ted Lieu of California.

Mr. LIEU. Thank you, sir, for your courage and for testifying before the United States Congress, and thank you, Chairman Royce, for holding this important hearing and giving us the opportunity to ask questions.

You, sir, had mentioned elites in your testimony. You said you were one of the elites. How many people are we talking about in that category, would you say?

Mr. THAE. You mean in the total elites or only just diplomats?

Mr. LIEU. The total elites in North Korea, just a ballpark figure.

Mr. THAE. Oh, it is really difficult to give exact percentage of the elite group. But according to the recent survey, the North Korean society is a class society.

While there are three classes, the main ruling class is called core class and next is wavering class and the last one is hostile class, and according to the academic search by calculating the population of Pyongyang, the capital of North Korea, the experts are arguing maybe 25 percent of North Korean population belong to the core class and usually elite are chosen only from core class. To my impression, when we say about elite I think maybe less than 10,000, to my knowledge.

Mr. LIEU. And you, as an elite, clearly saw the truth, which is why you defected. Is your sense that most of the elites also see the truth? Or do you think most of them are brainwashed and don't really know what's going on?

Mr. THAE. North Korea is a very strange and unique system. For instance, if you are in high rank, that does not mean that you have more access to information.

For instance, inside North Korea the most powerful institution which controls every sector of life is guidance and organization of Department of Central Committee of Workers' Party of Korea.

There are around 300 or 400 people actually who control the whole North Korea. But do these people have access to outside information like me?

No, because there are only 10,000 diplomats—there are only 1,000 diplomats working in Foreign Ministry who have that kind of access to world news, for instance, all those—the newspapers or all these foreign magazines.

But the people who are working much higher in the ranks do not have any ability to access this kind of outside information. So even though you are in high rank that does not mean that you have the access of information.

Mr. LIEU. And if we could deliver information to the elites, do you think that would be enough? Or do you think we'd actually have to do what you said, just give a lot of information to the people?

Mr. THAE. I think—oh, that we should make a different contents which can be targeted for the different—you know, the people and class of North Korea.

For instance, there is not a sense of solidarity between the core class and the wavering or hostile. There is a kind of, you know, hidden hatreds between core class and hostile class because during the Korean War and before the Korean War actually their ancestors fought each other.

So that is why now the ruling class, or elite, in North Korean society are afraid of any kind of political revenge if there is any change of the system or if there is any sudden contingency in North Korean society.

So we should continue to deliver a kind of message that if they cooperate with the rest of the population to change the North Korean regime, then their future would be guaranteed.

For instance, America, together with South Korea, can control and prevent any political revenge, any physical revenge from those victims of Kim Jong-un.

So we should try to make a kind of accommodation of feelings and those, you know, the hatreds between elite class and wavering and hostile class. So that is the best way to make a change.

Mr. LIEU. Thank you. I appreciate it.

I yield back.

Chairman ROYCE. Thank you, Mr. Lieu.

We go now to Mr. Ted Yoho of Florida.

Mr. YOHO. Thank you, Mr. Chairman.

Ambassador Thae, good seeing you again. As you can see this is on TV. It's being broadcast here. If it is being broadcast here with the astuteness of the North Koreans being able to hack in, we can probably assume that if Kim Jong-un and his people wanted to watch they are watching us right now. So I am going to direct this probably more to them.

And, you know, it was brought up that he's getting his ICBMs and his military weapons to protect his regime and preserve himself.

And I would think that if any other country wanted to topple him they would have done it by now. So I don't think that is really an issue.

I think what we really need to focus on is bringing him to the table and have a diplomatic end to this nonsense—you know, building nuclear wars in the 21st century.

And I wanted to ask you, without having North Korea on the state sponsor of terrorism list, do you think that makes the sanctions less effective versus putting North Korea back on the state sponsor of terrorism list? What's your thoughts?

Mr. THAE. I think we should avail every bit possible of non-military options to stop North Korea's continuation of this process.

Mr. YOHO. And, in your opinion, if we put North Korea—being a diplomat from North Korea, if we were to put North Korea back on the state sponsor of terrorism list, do you think that would have more effect by other countries that you visited?

Mr. THAE. Absolutely.

Mr. YOHO. Okay. Let me ask you this. What kind of relationship does North Korea have on a diplomatic level with other countries? What did they focus on?

When you're in a country—when you were a North Korean diplomat and you were in the countries that you were in, was it a feeling of respect you got from another country or was it a feeling of tolerance—that they put up with North Korea?

Mr. THAE. Oh, for instance, as a diplomat working in United Kingdom, I was always instructed to use the British Government's North Korean policy of critical engagement and I always tried my best to convince the British Government to let them use their role to prevent any possible war scenario on the Korean Peninsula.

For instance, if there is a key reserve for exercise of the British military representative or a small personnel were always invited to take part in that war exercise and it is my job to visit the British Foreign Office and the defense ministry to convince them not to go to joint military exercises.

Mr. YOHO. Okay. So you focused more on military, whereas my experience has been with most Embassies from country to country they focus on trade, economies, building economies, and cultural exchanges. You're saying you just focused on military and don't attack us?

Mr. THAE. Of course. You know, for instance, there is almost not any trade relations between North Korea and Britain. That's why there is no point for me to build that kind of things.

But as for cultural exchanges, the British side tried to invite as many as North Korean civil servants to take part in English short-term training course and I thought that it will be helpful for North Korean elites to look around democracy and freedom in U.K.

Mr. YOHO. All right. But you didn't see many Embassies sending people to North Korea, did you?

Mr. THAE. Oh, some countries——

Mr. YOHO. Other Embassies.

Mr. THAE [continuing]. Some countries and some countries not.

Mr. YOHO. All right. I just want to do a brief review of history and, again, this is directed at the people of North Korea that may be listening to this.

You know, we had a war with Germany and Japan. We had a war with South Korea and Vietnam. A lot of people died. A lot of buildings got destroyed.

But there is a common denominator and that common denominator is war. But the other common denominator is trade. You know, so we fought these wars and at the end we are all big trading partners.

South Korea has a market economy. They are our sixth largest trading partner. Vietnam is a communist country that engaged in market economies. They are our sixteenth largest trading partner.

Germany and Japan are huge trading partners. And so what I would encourage the Kim Jong-un regime is don't go to war. If we are going to trade, let's just start trading now and do whatever we can to come to the negotiating table.

And that is what I would encourage them to do, and the illicit activities they do in their Embassies from wildlife trafficking and endangered species, you know, bring that to an end and let's just work on the trade.

Thank you for your time and I will see you at lunch.

Chairman ROYCE. Thank you.

We go now to Joaquin Castro of Texas.

Mr. CASTRO. Thank you, Ambassador, for your testimony today and for your courage to defect.

Before I ask you a question, I just want to make a quick statement for the historical record. Some have suggested that perhaps we should have taken or suggested—intimated that perhaps we should have taken military action before to stop North Korea's nuclear program.

But the problem with that is that post-911, once we were knee deep in two wars in Iraq and Afghanistan, the idea that the United States in 2006 or 2008 or 2009 was going to jump into another war in Asia I think seems very strange and unrealistic.

There has also been conflicting reports about North Korea's nuclear capabilities. So let me ask you very directly, what is your understanding of their ability to deliver a nuclear weapon to, say, Japan or South Korea, or beyond that?

Mr. THAE. Oh, North Korea has started its nuclear development from late of 1950s. So that means that North Korea spent several decades on completing this nuclear program.

So I think it is—we should admit that North Korea has reached this certain level of nuclear development and actually they are at the doorstep before final completion.

Mr. CASTRO. Do you think they can deliver a nuclear weapon to South Korea?

Mr. THAE. Oh, I am not quite sure whether they will definitely deliver or not. But if we see the current North Korean brainwashing education system, they are educating the North Korean military officers that they should blindly follow what Kim Jong-un instructs them.

Mr. CASTRO. Well, I guess let me ask you this, Ambassador. Are you certain that they can't deliver a nuclear weapon to South Korea?

Mr. THAE. I think if Kim Jong-un believes that his life is threatened, I think he can do anything as long as he has something.

Mr. CASTRO. Okay. What's your understanding of North Korea's abilities within cyberspace?

Their ability to attack on a cyber level the way the Russians have interfered with our elections, for example, and the way that North Korea purportedly interfered with Sony's systems and did a big data dump? What's your assessment of their cyber capabilities?

Mr. THAE. I do not have the exact information about the cyber attacking—you know, the network of North Korea. But what I have seen during my life in North Korea has a very good educational system to educate those cyber professionals.

Mr. CASTRO. So people are being trained in cyber very actively?

Mr. THAE. That's right, from middle school age. So North Korea has a very good educational system to do that.

Mr. CASTRO. Okay. In addition to China, which other world economies—which other nations are propping up the North Korean economy?

I know China makes up the lion's share of it. But in your experience, based on what you saw, what other countries are out there that are helping prop up this economy?

Mr. THAE. I think the first, China, and the—naturally, Russia is the second and Southeast Asian countries like Vietnam, Malaysia, and Thailand these, the geographically nearest countries are the number third trading partners of North Korea.

Mr. CASTRO. And with what kind of activities? What kind of goods or what kind of things are being traded? What kind of activity makes up?

Mr. THAE. Oh, North Korea are exporting most of its raw materials like coal, the iron ore, seafood—of these things to China and in return North Korea buying the highly—technologies and modern goods from China.

So I think North Korea's foreign trade is mostly dependent on China.

Mr. CASTRO. And then one last question for you. It's been many decades now since North and South Korea have basically been two separate distinct nations.

Supposing that the North Korean Government and society did crumble. Do you believe that North Korea and South Korea, being apart now for so long, could realistically reunify?

Mr. THAE. Yes, I think so because, you know, we share same language and same blood and same culture. North and South are—has been divided only for 70 years.

But what I learned after my arrival to South Korea I learned we have so many things in common. There is no problem for me to understand Chinese culture or system or language.

So I think it will be a very easy process to accommodate the North and South Korea if the two Koreas are reunified.

Mr. CASTRO. Thank you. And then just to bookend my comment from the beginning, I think that this debate over whether we take—we should have taken military action in North Korea earlier, perhaps a decade ago, really underlines the mistake of the Iraq War.

We went into the Iraq War believing that Saddam Hussein was developing nuclear capabilities that North Korea was actually developing. But we took no action there.

Without making a judgment about whether we should or should not have taken military action, I think the mistake of Iraq is made worse by that realization.

Thank you for your testimony today, Ambassador.

Mr. THAE. Thank you for your question.

Chairman ROYCE. Thank you. We go now to Adriano Espaillat from New York.

Mr. ESPAILLAT. Thank you, Mr. Chairman. Thank you, Ambassador, for your insightful testimony.

For many years, we heard of the hunger and famine impacting the North Korean people. What's the status of the hunger and is there any famine?

Often, when peoples are facing those kinds of very adverse conditions there is an instinct to dissent and to rebel. Is there—what's the status of the food situation in North Korea right now?

Mr. THAE. Before the 1990s, North Korea maintained a very effective ration system. At that time, everyone in North Korea enjoyed certain rations of the food every month.

But these days, this ration system is only available for the civil servants or, like, working in the ministries or army—armies or security forces.

And if we see the effect of this malnutrition and famine in North Korea for the past 20 and 30 years, now if we compare the general height of North Korean young children and South Korean young generation, there is even 10 centimeters gap between South Korean young generation and North Korean young generation.

So because of this long decade of malnutrition, even the physical toll of North Koreans are changing. So I think this clearly proves that this kind of, you know, malnutrition—famine are still severely going on in North Korea.

Mr. ESPAILLAT. You mentioned in your testimony about North Korea's forced labor and China benefits. Which are the other countries that benefit from forced labor and are there any particular areas or products that they are producing that we can identify and potentially boycott?

Mr. THAE. For instance, the North Korean workers are the main source of labor in Russia for their timber industry. In Russian society now there is no Russian wanting to work in that cold weather conditions in Siberia. It is North Korean workers who help Russia's timber industry and for the construction industry the main source of labor are from North Korea.

And if you see the Middle East countries like Kuwait or Arab Emirates, of these countries there are more than 50,000 North Korean workers are working in those countries, especially in construction building.

And if you see the countries in Africa like the Angola or Uganda now there are many North Korean medical teams working in very bad severe conditions of rural hospitals to earn the hard currency in those countries.

Mr. ESPAILLAT. Okay. What are the—beyond the Chinese and the Russian sphere of influence, are there any relationships between the North Korean Government and countries in the Western Hemisphere?

Mr. THAE. Yes, of course. North Korea has diplomatic relations and they are with almost all European countries except France and Estonia, and North Korea has 11 Embassies in Europe. That's why this proves that North Korea still has a vast network of diplomatic service in European countries.

Mr. ESPAILLAT. What about in Latin America and the Caribbean?

Mr. THAE. In Latin America, to my knowledge, now there are Embassies in five countries like Cuba, Venezuela, Mexico, Peru, and so on—that to my knowledge, yes.

Mr. ESPAILLAT. Okay. Finally, you mentioned that there are thousands of defectors in China and in South Korea and the need to protect them is paramount, and if they are sent back to North Korea they will be torture—submitted to forced labor.

What kind of pressure do you think should be exerted against China to prevent this from happening but also to protect defectors there in the mainland of China?

Mr. THAE. Before I traveled to America, I happened to visit one school in Seoul where they kept the children born by this sex exploitation in China.

The children in school in Seoul where I visited the children even cannot speak Korean languages. They only speak Chinese. They are the children born between the ladies who worked as sex slaves in China and with Chinese husbands.

So when these—the poor North Korean ladies arrive in South Korea and they brought back all those—the children they had with their Chinese husbands. But the status of the children are very poor because they—these children were not registered while they were in China——

Mr. ESPAILLAT. What kind of pressures do you think——

Chairman ROYCE. I am going to have to interrupt at this point.

Mr. ESPAILLAT. Thank you, Mr. Chairman.

Chairman ROYCE. We have very few minutes—very little time left. I am going to as if Mr. Garrett and if Mr. David Cicilline would join me at lunch immediately after—a lunch which we are supposed to be doing right now with our witness.

We are far past out of time and we have been asked several times to wrap this up. But we have had one person waiting in the queue for a while who has a problem with his knee and that is Mr. Gerry Connolly from Virginia.

Gerry, would you like to ask your questions? And then the rest of us are going to go to lunch with this guest.

Mr. CONNOLLY. Thank you, Mr. Chairman, and I'll try to be succinct.

Mr. Thae, you indicated that essentially Kim Jong-un and his regime are going to pursue nuclear-tipped ICBMs at all cost because they see it as the key to the preservation of the regime.

Is there anything the Western alliance—the United States working with Japan and Korea and maybe—South Korea and even China or whoever—do we possess something he wants so much that he would stop the nuclear development and possibly even roll it back the way we did with Iran?

Mr. THAE. I don't think so.

Mr. CONNOLLY. So we are way past the point of no return?

Mr. THAE. That we should continue the current—the momentum of sanctions and campaign of diplomatic isolation. I think that is the only way to force North Korea to give up its nuclear ambition.

Mr. CONNOLLY. Sanctions don't have the appreciable effect because of the black market economy both through China and Russia that you were describing as well as some other business relationships North Korea has been able to establish. Is that your view?

Mr. THAE. Oh, but, you know, only sanctions is not effective to stop this process. But if we build up our pressure on China to stop the smugglings and also if we continue and expand our activity of disseminating information to educate the North Korean people, in the long run I am absolutely sure that North Korean people one day will stand up to change the course.

Mr. CONNOLLY. Do you—a final question—do you believe Kim Jong-un and his regime understand that the use of nuclear weapons would almost certainly bring enormous retaliation in kind, destroying the regime he seeks, purportedly, to perpetuate?

Mr. THAE. I think Kim Jong-un is aware of that but meanwhile, he also believes that if he has these nuclear weapons he can successfully compel Washington to pull its troops out from Korean Peninsula.

Mr. CONNOLLY. Thank you. I am going to yield back my time. I thank the chairman for his graciousness.

Thank you, Mr. Thae, for your courage and thank you for being here today.

Mr. THAE. Thank you.

Chairman ROYCE. Thank you, Mr. Connolly.

And Mr. Thae, I want to thank you for sharing your story and your insights with the committee here and also thank the National Endowment for Democracy, which has supported your trip.

As Ranking Member Eliot Engel said, we have had many hearings with experts on North Korea. No one has brought the insights that you have brought today and your testimony will be of great and lasting value, I believe, to the committee.

One area I wanted to underscore is the abysmal human rights situation of the North Korean people. We know how badly North Koreans are abused. Hundreds of thousands are in gulags.

The Kim regime's aggression against us reflects their aggression against North Koreans and I think one message we have heard again and again is the importance of communicating with the North Korean people, letting them know of the true nature of the brutal and very corrupt regime there.

And I think the Korean people deserve so much better than the government that they have and to that end we need to do a much better job with our international broadcasting efforts and other efforts.

I think our national security depends on it and, Mr. Thae, we appreciate your courage. Again, in appearing before us you have presented outstanding testimony that will help all Korean people and the cause of peace. You should be proud.

And the hearing stands adjourned.

Mr. THAE. Thank you.

[Whereupon, at 12:47 p.m., the committee was adjourned.]

APPENDIX

FULL COMMITTEE HEARING NOTICE
COMMITTEE ON FOREIGN AFFAIRS
U.S. HOUSE OF REPRESENTATIVES
WASHINGTON, DC 20515-6128

Edward R. Royce (R-CA), Chairman

November 1, 2017

TO: MEMBERS OF THE COMMITTEE ON FOREIGN AFFAIRS

You are respectfully requested to attend an OPEN hearing of the Committee on Foreign Affairs to be held in Room 2172 of the Rayburn House Office Building (and available live on the Committee website at http://www.ForeignAffairs.house.gov):

DATE: Wednesday, November 1, 2017

TIME: 10:30 a.m.

SUBJECT: An Insider's Look at the North Korean Regime

WITNESS: Mr. Thae Yong-ho
                   (*Former Deputy Chief of Mission. Embassy of the Democratic People's Republic of Korea in the United Kingdom*)

By Direction of the Chairman

The Committee on Foreign Affairs seeks to make its facilities accessible to persons with disabilities. If you are in need of special accommodations, please call 202/225-5021 at least four business days in advance of the event, whenever practicable. Questions with regard to special accommodations in general (including availability of Committee materials in alternative formats and assistive listening devices) may be directed to the Committee.

COMMITTEE ON FOREIGN AFFAIRS
MINUTES OF FULL COMMITTEE HEARING

Day __*Wednesday*__ Date __*11/01/2017*__ Room __*2172*__

Starting Time __*10:31AM*__ Ending Time __*12:47PM*__

Recesses __*0*__ (____to____) (____to____) (____to____) (____to____) (____to____) (____to____)

Presiding Member(s)
Chairman Edward R. Royce

Check all of the following that apply:

Open Session ☑
Executive (closed) Session ☐
Televised ☑

Electronically Recorded (taped) ☑
Stenographic Record ☑

TITLE OF HEARING:
An Insider's Look at the North Korean Regime

COMMITTEE MEMBERS PRESENT:
See attached.

NON-COMMITTEE MEMBERS PRESENT:
N/A

HEARING WITNESSES: Same as meeting notice attached? Yes ☑ No ☐
(If "no", please list below and include title, agency, department, or organization.)

STATEMENTS FOR THE RECORD: *(List any statements submitted for the record.)*

SFR - Representative Connolly
QFR - Representative Titus

TIME SCHEDULED TO RECONVENE __________
or
TIME ADJOURNED __*12:47PM*__

Full Committee Hearing Coordinator

HOUSE COMMITTEE ON FOREIGN AFFAIRS
FULL COMMITTEE HEARING

PRESENT	MEMBER	PRESENT	MEMBER
X	Edward R. Royce, CA	X	Eliot L. Engel, NY
X	Christopher H. Smith, NJ	X	Brad Sherman, CA
	Ileana Ros-Lehtinen, FL		Gregory W. Meeks, NY
X	Dana Rohrabacher, CA	X	Albio Sires, NJ
X	Steve Chabot, OH	X	Gerald E. Connolly, VA
X	Joe Wilson, SC	X	Theodore E. Deutch, FL
X	Michael T. McCaul, TX	X	Karen Bass, CA
X	Ted Poe, TX	X	William Keating, MA
X	Darrell Issa, CA	X	David Cicilline, RI
	Tom Marino, PA		Ami Bera, CA
X	Mo Brooks, AL	X	Lois Frankel, FL
X	Paul Cook, CA	X	Tulsi Gabbard, HI
X	Scott Perry, PA	X	Joaquin Castro, TX
	Ron DeSantis, FL	X	Robin Kelly, IL
	Mark Meadows, NC	X	Brendan Boyle, PA
X	Ted Yoho, FL	X	Dina Titus, NV
X	Adam Kinzinger, IL	X	Norma Torres, CA
X	Lee Zeldin, NY	X	Brad Schneider, IL
X	Dan Donovan, NY	X	Tom Suozzi, NY
	James F. Sensenbrenner, Jr., WI	X	Adriano Espaillat, NY
	Ann Wagner, MO	X	Ted Lieu, CA
X	Brian J. Mast, FL		
X	Brian K. Fitzpatrick, PA		
X	Francis Rooney, FL		
X	Thomas A. Garrett, Jr., VA		

Statement for the Record
Submitted by Mr. Connolly of Virginia

The North Korean regime's drive to become a nuclear power presents a real and dangerous threat to U.S. national security and that of our allies. Our priority must be to de-escalate tensions on the Korean Peninsula by providing steady leadership, reassurance for our allies, and a comprehensive strategy for denuclearizing the Peninsula. For North Korea, there must be some reward for compliance and cooperation with international nonproliferation efforts. Otherwise, we are stuck with a policy of talking loudly and carrying a big stick. The Trump Administration's "strategic chaos" is destabilizing an already volatile situation with bellicose rhetoric, uninformed and conflicting messages, and attacks on our allies.

With tensions flaring on the Korean Peninsula, President Trump warned that he would meet North Korean threats with "fire and fury like the world has never seen." But frankly, his response looks more like fecklessness and failure. The President appears to be singularly focused on military solutions to this intractable global flashpoint on the Korean Peninsula. His administration has proposed dramatic increases to the defense budget offset by an evisceration of our diplomatic capabilities, and he has failed to make key diplomatic appointments, including an Ambassador to Seoul and an Assistant Secretary for East Asian and Pacific Affairs. The President's inflammatory rhetoric and failure to resource U.S. diplomatic efforts are more likely to blunder us into war than set the stage for peace.

Now, it is more important than ever to stand strong with our allies, especially South Korea and Japan, and project a unified front. Amidst this extreme volatility on the Korean Peninsula, Trump has undermined the U.S. commitment to the U.S.-Korea Free Trade Agreement (KORUS), and criticized South Korea for its "talk of appeasement with North Korea." In September, I joined my fellow co-chairs of the Congressional Caucus on Korea to write to the president and rebuff him for opening fissures in the U.S.-ROK alliance – an alliance forged in blood – which has served U.S. security interests in the region and acted as a guarantor for the safety of 50 million South Koreans.

Following the most recent nuclear test, Trump suggested ending all trade with countries doing business with North Korea. Around 80 countries traded with Pyongyang in 2016, including China, Russia, India, Pakistan, Singapore, Germany, Portugal, France, Thailand and the Philippines. If the U.S. ended trade with China alone, we would forego 4.4 percent of U.S. GDP, compared to just 0.92 percent lost due to the Great Recession in 2008. Cutting off trade with 80 nations is an empty threat.

In August 2017, the President enacted the Countering America's Adversaries Through Sanctions Act (P.L. 115-44), which is the strongest sanctions regime ever passed by Congress. This hard-fought measure updates and expands the North Korea Sanctions Policy Enhancement Act of 2016 (P.L. 114-122) that was enacted last year. It authorizes new sanctions to restrict the use of North Korean exported labor, correspondent banking, and trade in oil, textiles, and food and agriculture products. The bill included my amendment, which will ensure that U.S. sanctions against North Korea do not impede the provision of vital U.S. assistance to developing countries for maternal and child health, and disease prevention and response.

U.S. sanctions are a necessary but insufficient tool to address the threat of North Korea's weapons program. The United States must undertake a rigorous diplomatic effort to urge the global community, and China in particular, to fully enforce international sanctions on North Korea. On September 11, the U.N. Security Council unanimously passed UNSCR 2375 against North Korea in response to its latest nuclear test. The resolution reduces Pyongyang's oil/petroleum imports by thirty percent, bans all textile exports, and prohibits new work permits for North Korean workers.

The Korean Peninsula remains one of the most dangerous flashpoints on the globe, and efficacy, above all else, must drive our efforts to defuse the North Korean nuclear threat. I look forward to hearing from our witness regarding how the United States may be able to incentivize the North Korean regime to denuclearize.

Question for the Record Submitted to
Mr. Thae Yong-ho
By Representative Dina Titus
On November 1, 2017

Question: Mr. Thae, thank you for your courage in coming to testify today. Reuters reported last night that the U.S. is quietly pursuing direct diplomacy with North Korea via the "New York channel," but on the public level we have not seen an improvement in relations. Based on your understanding of the Kim regime, which should we believe is the more accurate indicator of where the relationship is going—the public nuclear and missile test saber rattling or the private diplomatic dialogue?

Response: The Kim Jong un regime wants to complete its goal of acquiring an ICBM tipped with a nuclear warhead which can reach the US continent. Kim Jong un believes that he can scare American forces out of the Korean peninsula once he has that ability.

www.ingramcontent.com/pod-product-compliance
Lightning Source LLC
Chambersburg PA
CBHW080815280726
48660CB00018B/3456